FLEXIBLE BONES

Camino del Sol

A Latina and Latino Literary Series

FLEXIBLE BONES

POEMS BY
MARIA MELENDEZ

THE UNIVERSITY OF ARIZONA PRESS

TUCSON

The University of Arizona Press

© 2010 Maria Melendez

All rights reserved

www.uapress.arizona.edu

Library of Congress Cataloging-in-Publication Data
appear on the last printed page of this book.

Publication of this book is made possible in part by the proceeds of a permanent endowment created with the assistance of a Challenge Grant from the National Endowment for the Humanities, a federal agency.

Manufactured in the United States of America on acid-free, archival-quality paper.

15   14   13   12   11   10   6   5   4   3   2   1

For John

CONTENTS

II

PROLOGUE

[T]he bones of a bat's fingers have adaptations that promote bending. . . . making them less apt than ordinary bone to splinter under stress.

—Adam Summers, "Biomechanics," *Natural History,* February 2003.

BRIDGE

There's a ghost, ghost, ghost

      in my navel, navel, navel,

there's a ghost, ghost, ghost

        in my bridge.

There's a bridge, bat, bunker

      in my hundred-dollar bill,

there's a debt accumulating

        on my lawn.

There's a long time coming

      to my daughter's birthday party,

there's a mall evaporating

        with the dew.

There's a family in the middle

of the question, "How are you?"

"How's your mess?" It's no Iraq . . .

but it will do.

There's a reason, reason, reason

for the rake rusting outside,

there's a treasonous e-mail

in my inbox.

There's a balance sheet, a boulder,

and a "p" for "prophecy"

making ghosts out of the bushes

and the trees.

BEHIND EVERY GOOD SOLDIER

It sounds too scripted, unbelievable now,

but he really did ask: what would you think of me

if I killed someone? When this childhood

sweetheart joined the Marines,

I was back from college and leaping at him

for a week or so, smoking at his kitchen window, drinking

in the ridiculous brilliance of a typical

Berkeley garden, azaleas and tropical whatnot.

How sure of greenness it all seemed,

how shocking the mob of growing things

that surged against his little yellow house.

    —the answer I gave

evaporates, but the question roosts

in the mind's cave, elaborates rubbery wings

each time I meet a returning veteran.

Old lover, neighbors, boys marching drills

on the college quad, what do I think of you

when I think of you killing?

I see an old ghost, fatigued as storm-

blown sand, standing behind you, and it's

nothing but fangs and finger bones, disguised as a girl

with a sweet little honey-pot country

you've got to defend; she's got her dirty

little hands all over your weapons.

ARS POETICA:
AUTUMN PACKING LIST

A flock of meetings

A threat of oranges

A moon of matings

A crate of bells.

A gyp of whiskey

A drop of talent

A plate of pyrite

A fay of mist.

A hit of blood

A whiff of summer

A lisp of theory

A tuft of sea.

A weight of weasels

A pane of peacocks

A roll of bat wings

A bomb of leaves.

FOR ALL THEIR DISEMBODIED NAMELESSNESS, THEY SURE DO TALK A LOT.

for Gina Franco

She wants to crawl into a cave and wait for her breath to catch up with her. Breath on the mirror, breath on the sidewalk, breath on her hands. Bus breath. Book breath. Formal breath, known in academic circles as balustrade breath. *Aire de cuevas*, it's an illness, they say. When you have the *aire*, cave-breath, they say you can't stop wheezing. They say your voice melts into a sticky layer that coats your floor, like guano—commodifiable, potentially cosmetic. They say blessed are the breathless

                & the emptied out,

                for they shall inherit

                as a billows, as a bowl.

                For they shall respire

                on pure flame.

TO HOPE

for Christian Peacemaker Teams & Langley Hill Friends Meeting

As though sunlight couldn't kill you.

As though sex couldn't kill you.

    As though books had never been covered
                with human skin.

    As though otters thrive in the Tigris.

As though peace lay dormant in marsh mud.

    As though Tom Fox were made of clay
              and could be re-made.

If draught, therefore taproot.

    If cracked bridge, therefore bat roost,

pups by June. (If communion,

    therefore last supper.) If lasting hunger,

    then nightly flights. Half a million

Mexican free-tails flew east, above the river,

    spiraling out as though they'd never eaten.

I

AGING GODDESS SEEKS COMPANION, UNDERSTUDY

Our Lady of Morning Breath blows into her hand and sniffs—odor of last night's cigarettes, and the taste of sex she hasn't had yet, mix with the pasty smell of old blood; her sensitive gums acting up again. She consults her Day Planner, a crow perched on the iron lip of a music stand in the corner. "You lazy ho," he pants, "don't you know what time it is?" Now that stings. She's sluggish, maybe. Turtlish. Burdened by time. But Our Lady is not lazy, she's In Recovery from years as the heavy G's bag bride; life without crystal's a sludge-and-mud agony, some days. Not to mention chronic fatigue and mercury poisoning, asthma's large hand flexed to compress her chest every second the AQI pushes 140. Ten a.m. and already this summer day's thick with particulates. She thinks she's doing pretty goddamned well, all operative poisons considered. From birth, she has felt the smack of every hour vibrate along her slack muscle fibers. Hell yeah she knows what age, what era, what stage of the drama it is.

In a self-righteous hacking fit she coughs up soil and mineral grit, along with thirteen shriveled corn kernels, from which she divines a to-do list: worry if food can be both transgenic and traditional. Worry about who will sanctify the slag heaps of gold and uranium mines, who will die for the eco-sins of "the industrial world."

She spits on the seeds, rubs them between her rough palms to get the flip-side of their message: stop snorting lines of anxiety to feed your destruction jones. Get with a fifteen-year-old virgin with flexi-bones; roll her like a stunt horse in the dust. Place your tongue at the rusty source of her underground springs—then take her shopping for a new serpent skirt, a necklace of skulls.

CHILAM BALAM IN THE NEW MILLENNIUM

(Sacramento Valley)

I

Battered by winter, the long-legged

lampposts

swayed as though some Valentine

message plastered on their poles

made them shiver.

No shoe-shine boys on these streets,

this air-in-the-soles tennies town

was a ballet posing perfection,

a manufacturing location

for, "What is wholesome?"

It didn't smell like abuse

when a tentative winter sun rose

over our homes,

but no amount of organic produce

could brace us for the summer medicine show

put on by particulates:

breathe in, breathe out,

slow, killing breaths.

By then, the sun

& further stars detected

our fear by its electrical

interference: streetlights

flickered and dimmed as

cyclists

spun their alloy rims

on night-rides home,

danger draping invisible lines

across our faces

like spiders' threads.

If you really want peace,

a Muslim man said,

(this was a Sunday

in August, 03,

when 18 inches of heat fell

in less than three hours,

no breeze to blow it away),

if you really want peace.

He leaned forward into

the steady gaze of Unitarians

waiting in their pews:

then you must give

no less than your lives

no less than all your possessions,

no less than your fortunes and your families,

no less than the people of Iraq and Afghanistan

have already given.

II

It was the era

of the impotent grizzly

headless deer

blind elephant

crippled donkey.

Even at night

barn owls cowered,

not slipping out

in search of prey.

No priest or fortune-teller could read the signs,

stars so dim we tried not to fall in

drought-scoured ditches

flooded with shadows.

III

Without condors to clean up this mess,

without gods who make death their business—

well, there's always a turkey vulture waiting, somewhere.

Those buzzards love the suburbs.

IV

And what was that Valentine message?

Valentina, the dead revolutionary,

lives in her broken street songs.

Feb. '03 we walked into the streets

of a neighboring city, and our children

shouted for peace

as though it were the worthiest

soccer team. "Go back to Davis,"

some pickup truck shouted to us.

But the town was already abandoned,

peace extracted and divided

into pocket-sized packets

for later distribution at

promotional events.

And there was no repose for the children,

drug around by their wrists

from café to café

for the grown-ups' strategy meetings.

V

Oh there is a conqueror coming.

Oh death, we knew it was you,

with your thousand invisible fingers

itching

to pull that one trigger.

THE SKULL OF ARLEN SIU

The calavera of Arlen Siu
        wants coffee.

Relieved of being pretty,
        she laughs and laughs.

Revolutionaries march her face,
        enbannered,

down the avenida. Who carries off
        her clavicle, toes, and elbows?

The symphysis of shadesong
        hinged in her pubis.

        Volcanic birds, volcanic trees,
          volcanic economy . . .

The calavera of Arlen Siu
        wants fair-trade darkness.

Wants the universe to collapse back
        to knuckle-bone size.

Underground, every pound of dirt's prized
        for its infinite beauty spots.

GOOGLING GUADALUPE

(a little ranchera number)

Here's links to

a theme park in Texas,

a "cult" in L.A.,

and a weeping tortilla in Georgia;

oh, if Medjugorje

is just too far away,

don't be blue,

you can find her (and millions of other great items!) on eBay.

        That's right! I'm Googling the Virgin,

        I'm searching the Web

        for a lost goddess madre

        to sing me to sleep;

        I'm Googling the Virgin,

        I'm dragging the Net

        so that muchacha santa

        can show me the way.

Perhaps you knew her in childhood?

You could check classmates.com.

Is it possible she was that weird chick

in the starry blue dress at the prom?

I would not advise that you Ask Jeeves,

all he has are questions of his own.

It's as if he is virtually taunting:

"Where'd you think you would find her, cabrón!"

       ¡Híjole! We're Googling la Virgen,

       we're searching the Web

       for a lost goddess madre

       to sing us to sleep;

       we're Googling la Virgen,

       we're spinning the Web

       so that muchacha santa

       will not get away.

When your carpal tunnels start complaining

and your positas begin to itch,

then it's time to step back from the iMac

and hunt through the streets for that Lady.

Four times she showed at Tepeyac, y

parece que le gustan las flores,

so go make your power establishment

spread flower seeds instead of pavement.

        Yahoo! We're riding our motherboards,

        surfing the Web

        for a lost goddess madre

        to sing us to sleep;

        we're Googling the Virgin,

        we're searching World-Wide

        for a morena santa

        to show us the way.

THE FIFTH APPARITION: RENO

Out a casino basement like a Stone Age

mamacita on a suited man's arm, terra cotta

silk dress with only one shoulder strap, wide

like a hide curving off her back and down

across her ostrich-egg breasts—

Dare we number the feathered angels

and bare devils revolving in a waltz

on that slick shoulder ball?

(Faced with a modest blue

cotton shift, we might guess

her fate lay in giving, we'd

associate motherly verbs: bathe,

mollify, hallow, salve.) To hell

with egg-shaped, she's nobody's—

in that owning-it-all look

she tosses at the streets, in the

tall spikes tethered to her feet—

she offers no succor, no

slack mud to plow, she's out

to kill sweet things

that eat Her in pieces,

to kick in any

scavenging teeth.

OUR LADY OF CORPORATESPEAK

Real Estate bubbles

the skin at her throat,

and you know she gives

good overhead.

Says, "I am the nightmare

that powers you up,

the biggest dropped ball

of them all."

"I've visioned your skull

on the clacking row

of baubles

around my waist."

May her Total Quality endure

through the Achievement and Teamwork of her breasts!

Nicknamed "Win-Win,"

their Next Steps are

suckle and suffocate.

Struggle to work yourself out of the loop!

THIS IS AN AUTOMATIC REPLY

I will be out of the office   for rakish reasons

and will check all my   begonias' pulses

on my return.

You're sorry.   I'm welcome.

―――――――――

Check out my graffiti site: all the titty and vitamins

a growing sectarian needs!

―――――――――

You are not on my approved migraines list.
To get on my approved migraines list, just click
your glittery heels together three times, and say:

My face for your comb.
My face for your comb.
Blowfish or loam.

(the March mud's surge

& insurge)

KENT BROCKMAN, HERE, ON THE COMING OF THE NEW SUN.

Much of Springfield is abuzz about the upcoming changing of suns, and I, for one, welcome it. In fact, I've long suspected the outgoing sun of being a pallid imitation of a star, and couldn't be more thrilled to know that a real sun is on its way to feed us and heat us and drive us out of our old brains, into new ones.

Just a moment. I'm now getting word . . . the new sun has been delayed due to some confusion at Inter-Stellar Traffic Control. I have always been a loyal follower of the old sun—in fact, I hum "Hail to the Chief" every morning as I watch it rise, and suggest you do the same, giving the old sun, henceforth known as Daystar 1, the level of dignity and respect a flaming gaseous ball of its stature rightly deserves.

LOVE SONG FOR A WAR GOD

Every part of you contains a secret language.

Your hands and feet detail what you've done.

Your appetite is great, and like the sea,

you constantly advance, lunge after lunge.

Unlike my brother sleeping in his chair,

you do not take reality with ease.

Your pain builds up its body like a cloud

rotating a collage of hot debris.

O Teacher! We have learned that all men's tears

are not created equal. We were wrong

to offer flames to quell your fires. Still,

I must dismember you inside this song.

Your mouth's dark cave awaits Victory's kiss;

blood is the lid your calm eyes never lift.

EL VILLAIN

"I fled the West Coast to escape them, but I still see illegals

Everywhere," whines a letter-writer in our rural Utah paper,

Applauding a local ICE raid. "How does it feel to be a problem?"

Everyone (no one) wanted to ask Du Bois, circulating his elegant

Diction and mixed-race face among Atlanta glitterati, turn

Of the century, when the White Sixth Sense was "I can smell

Negroes and Jews." The question ices my hair and eyelashes,

All Raza one family of suspects in this age of round-ups; am I

To breathe in prejudice, breathe out light? How does it feel

To be a problem? Some well-meaning White ones want a Christ of

Me, sacred heart on display. "Where are your documents

Naming this pain?" They hope for a nibble of rage. I see Lourdes,

Seven years old and *sin documentos*, embrace my daughter hello,

Good-bye, every day on their school's front steps, the two of them

Giddy with girl pacts. When Lourdes solves subtraction problems,

Safe at her dim kitchen table, how does her mother, Elva, feel,

As her daughter works a language that will never add up to home?

Down the street, I see Rodolfo from El Salvador, legal refugee, dance

The glee of a Jazz victory in front of his big screen. Ask him how

Pupusas feel in his mouth, corn-dough communion with *patria*. His wife,

Inez, is fourth-generation Mexican American from Salt Lake City.

                              Fuck these pedigrees. How does it feel

For Rodolfo, Inez, Elva, Lourdes, me, to be seen as not-quite-right,

Not quite US, not from around here, are ya?

I will not say. I will not display our stigmata.

We shouldn't need papers to cross from familia to politics.

Ask the seer-of-illegals, the maid of ethnic cleansing,

How it feels to hold a broken feather duster.

TOPAZ TRIPTYCH

re-truthed versions of articles from the Spring, 1943, Topaz Times, *published in central Utah's Topaz Internment Camp*

TIME GIVEN TO REVISE 'NO' REPLY TO QUESTION 27

If you will not give your lives for US

if you will not climb, with your wife's

last kisses still wet on your lips,

into US' flying death boxes and

explode a message in the sky

that sky their sky if you will not

parse skies with US it may be inter-

preted by some that you've spit

US out of your mouth like a bitter

seed we prefer you think of US

as tiny machines, grinding loyally

in your cells, we urge you see

US as dear and built-in cell mach-

ines and advise against calling

US' advice "orders," we recom-

mend the term "signals" and trust

you can tell a signal from a no

-ise.

AMFP SEEKS PART AND PARCEL

The American Museum of Fixed
Patterns hopes you'll keep your eyes
on the ground, hopes you'll send
your children dust-ward, kindly
queries you for help in herding
cracked or sherded bits of culture
from underfoot, under-shack, scurry
them back to our hungry gazes.
No, they're not ours yet, but they're
waiting in the hot soil to be lifted
from their loose-grained state of
historical drift, to be freed of un-
ownership. Realizing that certain
conditions in the Safety Centers
are detrimental to the

for generations to come, AMFP
looks forward to awaits calculates
banks on foresees your faithful particip-
ation in this effort may uplift some
flagging spirits.

BIRTH OF FIRST PRIZE PUPPIES IN TOPAZ CLAIMED

A unique "first" for
Topaz was claimed by Mr.
and Mrs. K. Ito, 9-6-B,
whose English Fox Terri-
er gave birth to 2 pups
last week. The register-
ed names of the 2 new-
comers are "Debutante of
Topaz" and "Desert Beau-
ty of Topaz." They are
descended from "Norway
Saddler," a champion who
has won 56 blue ribbons
in National Dog Shows. Mr.
and Mrs. could not be rea-
ched for comment, and
were last seen bu-
rying three stillborns
near the southwest fence.

II

CATAMITE

for Steven Cordova

At what point did you know heaven was full

of you?

Gay angels
striking their dandy poses
for Renaissance painters' stiff
brushes—

heaven open to your kind
even in the time
of Flores Man,

      with their mini-striving and mini-sex,
      mini-hunger and mini "true selves,"
      their mini-urge toward the Angel
      of Grapefruit-sized Brains—

Goddammit, I miss you.

Your Peoples' Republic
of Bklyn is 26 hours by train.

Why don't poets ever say
what they %$#@! mean?

_____

HIV

makes me want to know

the forecast date of your death; by when

should I be prepared

to live without you?

Hubris and blindness and the furnace

of external tragedy (warming my insides like liquor, sorry

to say)

makes me assume that you'll

go before me—

If I made a habit of saying what I meant,

I'd give you this:

under the press of sunlight, I felt desperate

to take your arm and walk to forever

as we exited the Basilica that day.

———————————————————

Who else do I know that could say,
This. Place. Is so! Gay.
—and let his calm voice ricochet
off the cherubs adorning the topaz dome
and the stations, carved 14 ways
of transmitting guilt—Christ
can't help but crack a smile under the force
of all your daring, all your truth.

Where do you get the strength to be you?

Brother dear, my fellow sister—
I know spraying your name in the face
of each day, a tagger marking your
whole path "gay," isn't heroism,

it's the only way

to live without shutting the doors of your heart.

You told me the slur

your boss drooled out, a new one

for you, an old one from The Book.

Cata-what? According to Webster's Online,

it's spelled   𝍎 𝍎 𝍎 𝍎 𝍎 𝍎 𝍎   in Dancing Men,

means a boy kept for unnatural purposes.

Oh! We chuckled,

we had a nice laugh,

that's a good one.

We were ex-Catholics on tour

of sanctuaries we'd never kneel in

willingly.

—what do we carry

as holy?

A lock of hair

from the monster of human loving,

beautiful monster of night—

a bottled note

of Cavafy's laughter,

a measure of voice

that resembles the heart's

first flutter,

and the power to shimmer our light

all the way out

to the angels, waiting

with heat-white drapes eternally beginning

to drop from their fulsome buttocks.

TERESA

The washcloth has failed

to notice, the socks and the hairbrush

don't see

       that although I used what God

gave me

      (drew a husband in, grew

          some children, basic

            recipe)

I think of myself as male.

           Does anyone ask the age of the spirit

           shivering inside the box elder tree?

           Who will seek the shape of clouds

           disguised within clouds?

AN OCEAN OF CODE

I want to disappear like the glaciers.

    To hear the story I've misnamed "mine"

        drip, like time, back into

            pebbly soil. Trying

to decipher who wrote these praises,

    spoke with crows, who made

        this dent in mystery, solving

            for pattern, I break

a book spine with my foreign-

    sounding name on it . . . find nothing

        but type and the same head-haze.

            The furthest out of the fog

I can lumber, today: spit-shining

    a smudge of food off my daughter,

        my thumb rubbing wet circles

            on her cheek.

A bald eagle fledges from a bare

    cottonwood on the elk refuge,

        eyeing the coyote crunching

            a yearling calf's carcass—

and on the plains, a wave

    of one thousand cranes ululate con-

        volute calls, gaze from the Eocene

            age to the dusky Platte muds.

A better poet would know

           what it means, all of it—clattering song,

                    the keel of it, the bloodied, scavenging

                            teeth of it—I'm deaf on the floor

of an ocean of code, but still

           something globes, bubbles,

                    floats from my lips,

                            rising to riddle the surface.

[UNTITLED]

Everywhere, I am talked to by silence.

    Who do you think you're kidding?—it says.

    And—Chrissakes, give me break.

Apparently, silence has no problem swearing.

    Meanwhile, uncurling leaves burble

        like springs, or grate and squeal

        as metal train wheels;

    the sun alone hears leaf-birth

        the way bees can see u.v.,

            the way snakes sense dimensions of heat.

            What sensory spectrum is our specialty?

        The ear's guess-work, the heart's deep fabrications—

KNOT OF PRAYER

For the Buddha with his hand

            down a little girl's pants

For the Christ who is fondling

            her nipples

For the Heavenly Father settling

            her fingers on his shaft

For the Ever, Everywhere

            forcing into—

Be gone, be gone, be gone, be gone, gone beyond beyond.

        The gasping furnace, the rasp
        and clatter of face-wide leaves
        scattering over the deck—we've
        learned to move through
        our new home's armory of sounds
        without alarm, taming
        jumpiness with mental labels:
        a creaking here, a scratching there,
        it's Normal, Natural.

We make a custom of raking,

get used to the heat system's

raucous breath. I kill

and kill the same spider,

big hobo in the tub,

every morning—one

click forward in the mom-lock

of rituals turned each day

to block the children

from threat, the various venoms.

       Next house over lives a code

          violation, a criminal

        record, an offender under

       watch by State Corrections.

       More than all the protective charms

       and spells I wish I knew, I wish

       I were a perfect guardian

       beyond exhaustion every night—

       three doors to check before sleep

       and I'll forget one, guaranteed—

       one of these nights, I'll forget.

What could be tied and waiting / at the stake?

My curled, my jumping

girl, six years of hair-

brushing, brother-

chasing, tiny one who sings into the face

of a stuffed tiger, she of cheeks

soft as sage leaves . . .

Home-page for the registry

lists his targets:

Female, Child.

Home-page advises: be a good

neighbor, do not harass, offer

acceptance, support re-entry.

Such a sticky state!—asked to act as though

it's human!

This tearing and breakage, this . . .

him.

He likes to smoke on his porch step
across from my window.
He's out there every night
while I'm washing dishes.

A compassionate person would ask

what went wrong to make him act this way?

I am not compassionate.

I am afraid—

to worship the Greatness
when It stains the edge of soothing nights
with sunlight meant to scald.

For the Roshi implacably asking me
to let monsters live in peace,

For the Apostles reminding me
to love my neighbor,

For the Hierarchs keeping quiet
about monsters in their midst,

For the Cosmos' random collisions

        launching life,

      I clamp my teeth on this plea
      for selective banishment—for the halves of you
      that say it's damage that teaches,
      keep your half-hands the hell
      away from my girl.

      In the hot gold of autumn,
      he mows the back lawn and talks to her—
      we've only lived here two weeks.

      You can get used to anything. 14 pounds
per square inch pressure on your face ("one atmosphere"),
the 12-pound melon at the end of the stalk of your neck.

          I tell the kids "don't talk to him" and "run,"
          now seeing him is more fun
          than a sprinkler.

I have been so angry
at my children
that my teeth clatter,

a fist

within me

rattles my frame

as it fights to be

renamed.

I dreamed it was meth

        that did it, "thirteen years ago,"

and I dreamed his regret. He

        said, "That was

not me, not me." It was his face

        entering this plea,

as a prisoner who's hunched before a judge.

        His weathered cheeks, same

ash-blond hair, his mouth moving,

        but my voice.

One wants one's response to be firm,

immobile, frozen. As a mother, I have planned

to be consistent. Lord, let this fear
keep clenched in me, tight as February
buds grip their green secrets. Let me not
relax into blossom, Lord, unfold me not
unto your holy weathers.

Maybe other universes have flat
refugia, homages to stasis, planets
sure of their places. Not ours,
with its rotatious whirl and
orbit, we get tipped into July
every time.

Summer instructs us
            in patience. Be still
            and float over
            afternoon fever—
                  night air will race through
                  to loosen ribbons
            that braided heat tight
            against the day.

A corpse, however wounded,

joins the root world, gets used to

the formative earth's

manifold pressures.

We're not used to that man, but he grows

spectacular vegetables.

My husband accepts

an armful of sweet onions—

"Come and pick plums anytime."

(Even the moon goes home and shuts her door

when her work in the garden's through.)

For the moon with her tongue

in the unwashed pans,

in the spider's jaws,

in the girl's ear—

DESIRE OF DAYSPIRIT TO BE SEEN

I roused you from the deep sleep of nonbeing.

However you intend to answer me,

    I will walk in your door,

                    spread my arms,

    and their curtains of flame

    will unroll to the floor.

There have been signs: I can't retreat.

    You watch the moon from your bed

        and suddenly think of me—

("desire," in your words, "to touch who is not there").

    The moon shudders

      as it crosses through the threads I've hung between us

   & brightens to its full, reflective glare,

which means, somewhere, the sun

      has not forgotten you.

Each time a horizon swallows its ball of light,

        you're not unsaved—

    I still blaze

into the space that webs all bodies,

      the one star close enough to sit a lit fuse

      in your blood.

AS WITCHES DO

for Yosefa Raz

"Jews don't usually describe G-d's hair,"
said my best poet-friend, an Israeli-Berkeleyan;

she was coaching me on how to know
a mortal addressee, in Hebrew poetry, from one divine.

"They usually won't claim to have seen His face."
With or without all due respect, I lay claim to it all.

I say I have seen the toenails, sucked the knuckles,
yanked a hank of the Author's hair, taboos be

damned (that's how we do), for what is Man
but that which G-d is doing at this time?

What is G-d's hair but broken brush?
We rip it from the sand—I've taken G-d

in my mouth, but refused to swallow.

MAÍZ DESMADRE

I. Smart Food for a Road Trip

Was it Donner pass, where we slid along the road in November snow?

A Buddhist hell, a world over-full of white, more flurries falling

in wet bundles. We munched on goods from crinkly plastic sacks,

comparing girlhoods. Amy brought chains, I brought the greasy snacks;

we tried a night drive back to Cali after three days thinking "wilderness"

at a conference in Nevada. What did we hope the Sierras would give us?

A break? A crack? A window? In a car close as a confessional,

we laid out stories of our fathers like faded trading cards,

examined their about-to-hit poses, and recited all their record-

breaking stats, letting the numbers spread their contaminant

fractions of rage. In Amy's grip, the steering wheel turned

dowsing rod, occasional tremors divining some kind of traction.

Tired of terror's muck and slush, we mined silence for a mineral

core that years of fear couldn't scratch. *Those bloody sharps and flats—*

a poet wrote—*those endless calamities of the personal past. Bah!*

She meant to ban them from the rest of her life; we knew how she felt.

Would we really weight our last moments with groaning panting hating

grieving? Near-death winter driving's no time for despond. I rolled

down the window just over the crest, chucked out a few puffs of Smartfood

White Cheddar Cheese Flavored Popcorn™. We give what we can, I said,

mock-gallant, wanting to get on the Great Something's good side without leaving the car, without stopping, of course. Thankfully,

the Divine, at times, accepts processed offerings. Came a valley,

soaked in rain, the safety of stillness. Luxury-stretching our necks

and legs. Did you see a beast step into our tracks

and put freezing lips to our sacrificial snack foods?

She could smell the salt from miles away, a starving deer on the move.

II. Synonymies

little deer / little serpent / little corn maiden / little green daughter

mujeres / maíz / atole (de masa, vainilla, canela) / breast milk

ca'ag / body / a world power / four million peasants

monsanto / techno-ag / terminate (not germinate) / $3.6 billion net sales

doorway / wind path / the great breath / pollination

pollination / creation / or transgenic contamination / who controls

what comes from the earth?

white corn / now I am / sown by hand / the First Action

red corn / now I am / stored / a portion of Time

dark corn / now I am / thrown to water / for divining

yellow corn / now I am / ground / body-to-be

III. "Desmadre" means "all mixed up."

In Puebla, in Guerrero, and Oaxaca—the first

state where genes from another species

(a cauliflower bacteria) were discovered

introgressed into native corn—Lilias, Adelas,

Olgas cook handmade tortillas by the millions

on stone *comales* every morning. I don't counsel

nostalgia for their ancient kneel and bend,

or worship of their skeletal damage at elbows

and shoulder balls. I don't want these

"peasants" to hold a pose for me.

What I want is to give these women

an un-contaminated wind, free of U.S.

pollen from transgenic maize imported

to their home *terrano* without their consent,

sold without labels or warnings.

U.S. engineers wrought corn ears

that grow no "smut," a fungal delicacy,

pesticide-ready breeds with leaves too small

for wrapping tamales, and the nightmare

semillas asasinas, trademarked seeds

that "terminate," rather than re-grow freely.

I don't mean to make brown women stand

for all suffering at corporate hands.

U.S. farmers who need reproductive

lines, corn eaters, corn-syrup

imbibers world-wide, all of us

men and women of maize, hurt

from the ramming through of GM corn

into forcibly opened markets. Popping, dent

red, *azul*, some Mexican varieties of maize specialize

in microclimates, one communal hillside's

tailored daughter, little mother. A little green

deer appears with the new corn, seven serpents

slide through as it grows, say the stories, say

corn was a gift, four spirit daughters sacrificed

themselves so our own daughters, corn

and human, could go on. Paleo-ecologists say

"selected from wild grass by Mesoamericans

over 6,000 years ago," how many synonyms

for *cuerpo* have been spun from the Americas'

ombligo, how many carefully nursed varieties

of He and She and We are now enlaced

within those coiled genes?

IV. Translexic Contamination: Mad-Libbing a Chant for Planting Corn

as recorded in Nahuatl

by Fr. Ruiz de Alarcón, 1629

translated into English

by Francisco X. Alarcón,

1992

nomatca nehuatl

nitlamacazqui

I myself

Spirit in Flesh:

tla xihualhuian

nohueltiuh

Tonacacihuatl

hear me, Tonacacihuatl

elder sister

Lady of Our Flesh

tla xihualhuian

Tlateuctli

hear me, Tlateuctli

Mother Earth

ye momacpalco

nocontlalia

nohueltiuh

Tonacacihuatl

on your open hand

I am setting down

my elder sister

Tonacacihuatl

frenetically modified

by Market Interests, early 2000s

I myself, Profit

Potential in Flesh

ask you open for me,

Tonacacihuatl, elder sister,

shopping mall of our flesh.

Reveal all the memos

pinned to your inner corkboard.

   (I'm dissecting

     my senescent sister,

     Tonacacihuatl.

     Don't get your skivs in a wad.

     Don't wail.

     Don't laugh at us.

     Tomorrow

     and the day after

     I want to stamp

     on the strands of snakes

     that twist in her seeds.)

Let me tattoo

fake stigmata

on your palms!

(I shall honor

the finger-

nails of my sister

as I yank them out.)

in English, it continues: *in Nahuatl, it continues:*

don't shame yourself   almo timopinauhtiz

don't grumble   almo tihuexcapehuaz

don't laugh at us   almo tihuexcatlatlacoz

tomorrow   cuix quin moztla

or the day after   cuix quin huiptla

I want to see again   in ixco icpac nitlachiaz

the face of my elder sister   in nohueltiuh

Tonacacihuatl   Tonacacihuatl

let her stand   niman iciuhca

on the ground   in tlalticpac hualquizaz

I shall greet   in nicmahuizoz

I shall honor   in nictlapaloz

my elder sister   in nohueltiuh

Tonacacihuatl   Tonacacihuatl

A LATINA POET CAN BE A GOOD DOG

, loyal, but not too licky, can be
a good parlor trick
if you ask her.

she can walk backward & beg,
speak on command
& roll over.

rage for one biscuit,
mythos for two.

a rip in her heart runs like a nylon tear,
right to the corner
of her two rosy lips.

a latina poet can be a grave
digger, a prophet,
a scourge, can arrange

blades of various eras
in your vase, man.

if it pays.

i'm saving up change
for a gorgeous bridge,

burying money like bones.

trained to display a flexagon
of opinions on all things flexican,

tap me in academic company
to be a tall, cool glass of chicana

lite, goes down easy. if i pimp out
a little cultura, who does it hurt?

my position on immigration
                              is missionary!

on cherríe moraga:
                              doggie, claro

que sí. on "i am
                              joaquín": sixty-

nine. on the juárez
                              murders: turtle.

---

where's there room in poetry
        for the elation and shame
            of accidentally

      throwing the right signs
          before temple veils, my pale
              skin parting the waters, my half-

                              breed ability to pass for friendly

                                    nearly canceling the risk

                                          of my last name?

                    _____

wáchale, inside-outside voices
calling me by my true and

fakish names: be careful where
you raise your leg and mark. i'm stretching

out my gait to work your scent-line, america,
i'm putting my mongrel bitch-nose to the trail.

ARS POETICA: FROM A DUSTY CALIFORNIO ARENA

Deep in my clocks,

my pockets, my days,

a bull has been fighting a bear.

Read:

space vs. time, right hand and left,

or see as money sees:

Damas y caballeros!

I give you wide and well-bred

gentleman's horns,

opposing the sow-wild earth.

Europe's finest bull! versus

the New World's angriest mother-

grizz. No—they're trapped

in a ring, and each wants to go home,

but the fanning, the egret

hats, waistcoats, and canes

won't stop 'til they've heard

death draw water,

won't leave 'til they've eaten

their ration of fear.

Here's where belief

in one Bear Nature gets us,

belief in blood

offered by name.

ANN'S ANSWER

after Ann Stanford

My best poet-friend finds an American quest for

                inner peace

abhorrent.

She thinks all our nails, in wartime,

         should be bitten down to bloody.

If the war seems far—

      all the more reason

        to rend our garments.

     And I say:

Those who can stain their hands

        with wild blackberries,

should.

Let those who remember the earnest part

       of heat and orchards,

the companionable crack

       of dry leaves under their feet,

let those called to answer cicada rustle

       over the marshy water

alone.

ARS POETICA: PLATANUS RACEMOSA

Here's *amor,* clawing the skin of sycamores—

track it by the jagged patches of bare trunk

exposed between pieces of broken bark.

                                                             Who should you ask

about the way love picks at the surface puzzle,

crunches away the discernable for the porous

inner wood? How did those "clever natives" know

boiled bark could treat a springtime wheeze?

A little trial and error, sure, but mostly,

the tree asked to be used that way.

                                                             We offend the unused

trees when we don't drink their remedies;

this love metaphor and its host, this sycamore,

are curatives for the loneliness that repeatedly opens up

between ourselves and the Creator; to learn of love,

go to love, its unsolved path on a crooked tree,

and all it has downed or dropped.

Kick the leaves

like parchment on the ground, shock the fat

black beetle with your thick toe,

rattle an inquest he can read, then listen

for what's asking to be written. I'm no expert,

but the beetle seems to say: breathe out through your skin,

feed off decay, and chew without redress—

Love breaks open the bark to feed itself

on what's exposed, while the gasping soil is fed

on what is shed. May language be an act of love.

ROASTING GRASSHOPPERS

for G.S.

First, to praise

the old cast-iron fry pan,

second, to praise the crunch.

Third to say Fear is no

Factor here:

just a small fire

in a basin of land,

Deep Time hunkered

in ridges and crests;

just a bony ring

cradling the eye.

Fourth to say wait for me

in campfire smoke,

fifth to say smoke waits for no one.

Sixth for your departed wife,

she could've stomached them all,

seventh, for leaving space . . .

The grasshopper eggs

bind eighth to themselves,

ninth for slim tunnels

they're laid in.

Tenth is your old teeth

testing them out,

tasting, and passing them on.

WESTERNER EXILED TO THE
AFFORDABLE MIDWEST COMES HOME

I thought my life was over and my heart was broken.
Then I moved to Cambridge.
—Louise Glück, *Vita Nova*

After years of my discernment organ's
failure, when tree after tree turned its
back to me and sighed, after seasons
of the whole earth's silent treatment:

I'm starting to believe in eagles again.
Gilbert Sorrentino said what's dead
in you is dead, don't trouble yourself
with trying to be whole. Just go

on down and visit those old parts
now & then. No. I was dead to leaves
and dead to sun, to feathers, beaks,
and seeds. But finally, we're moving;

while driving a life-loaded car
through a long curve on 89
out of the Wasatch, not having to be
jealous of people who say things like

"out of the Wasatch," I swear to dog

and coyote I started to scan the uplift,

the high, bare cliffs,

for whitewash below ledges, for nests.

NOTES

To Hope

March 10, 2006, Austin, Texas: Saw the famous flight of the pregnant bats from under the Congress Street bridge tonight. When I heard they'd found Tom Fox's body in Baghdad, I felt a wrenching regret over not praying hard enough for him during his disappearance. How self-centered of me, to respond to this loss with spiritual performance anxiety. He was killed in a world already swirling with prayers and waged peace because Light led him to it—not because he was guaranteed results. What a ridiculous miracle hope is. What a ridiculous miracle it should be asked of us.

Read Tom Fox's Iraq blog at http://waitinginthelight.blogspot.com/.

Chilam Balam in the New Millennium

In recognition of Christopher Sawyer-Lauçanno's version of the Mayan pre-Columbian masterpiece, *The Books of Chilam Balam*. The books combine prophecy, history, chronology, ritual, and mythology, and include foretellings of the chaos wrought by conquistador violence. In his introduction to *The Destruction of the Jaguar: Poems from the Books of Chilam Balam* (City Lights Books, 1987), Sawyer-Lauçanno points out that the Mayan prophet-poets use "history as a guide to the future." In traditional Mayan cosmology, events recur cyclically in the continuum of time.

The Skull of Arlen Siu

Arlen Siu (1957–1975) was an early martyr of the Sandinista movement in Nicaragua. Photos of a 1978 FSLN march, taken by Susan Meiselas, prominently feature Siu's face on a banner held by student protesters.

El Villain

FOUND POEM FEATURING INTERNET SEARCH RESULTS (1–10 OF 2,020) AND THE SIXTH CONGRESSIONAL RECORD

I see illegals as an invasion force coming here to take over the United States. The only course of action for the US Government is to enforce the current . . .

I see illegals in Prince Georges county using food stamps. I know they are illegals. I hear the conversations. I see them crowding into small apartments. . . .

At 6 AM I see illegals on bicycles coming to work at restaurants. The city does nothing to stop them and allow American kids to get the jobs. . . .

I would ask gentlemen whether, with all their philanthropy, they would wish to see freed slaves sitting by their sides deliberating in the councils of the nation? . . . would [they] have these people turned out in the United States to ravage, murder, and commit every species of crime?

I see illegals working, observe them on a daily basis, coming into the lunchroom from a filthy work environment, and walking past a hand washing station as . . .

Apparently in Mexico they never had the commercial with the crying Indian, because I see illegals throwing wrappers, cans etc out of their moving vehicles . . .

I get mad when I see illegals move in and can't get a job and start selling drugs, robbing people, stealing cars, etc. It's not right. . . .

Next day, I told the owner of the Wendy's that any time I see illegals, I'm not going to be eating in the same place—I don't want their diseases. . . .

The senator from Rhode Island said he was in hopes that every member belonging to the Northern States would see the impropriety of encouraging slaves to come from the Southern States to reside as vagabonds and thieves among them . . .

Well, usually when I see illegals working I tell them "I just called ICE." You should see their faces, they get totally upset—

I see illegals all the time. I've never trusted the fucking asians of all stripes. They saw our fertile convenience store market and struck while the . . .

i see illegals everywhere; on tv, in the gov, and all over this stolen continent. all white people and their descendants are the true illegals on this land.

(Italicized segments from *The Negro in the Congressional Record*, Vol. II, compiled and annotated by Peter M. Bergman and Jean McCarroll, Bergman Publishers, 1969.)

Topaz Triptych

The Topaz Internment Camp, located in central Utah, operated from 1942–1945 and held a peak population of 8,000. See http://topazmuseum.org. These poems were inspired by articles from the camp's official newspaper, the *Topaz Times*. Thanks to the Special Collections archives at Utah State University for access to their Topaz collection.

Catamite

Thanks to Eric Gudas, and to Jules Supervielle (tr. George Bogin) before him, for the phrase "beautiful monster of night."

Maíz Desmadre

See http://www.greenpeace.org/mexico/ and *"Mujeres de Maíz*: Women, Corn and Free Trade in the Americas," in *The Colors of Nature: Culture, Identity, and the Natural Word*, 2nd edition, ed. Alison Hawthorne Deming and Lauret E. Savoy

(Milkweed Editions, 2010). See also *Zapotec Science: Farming and Food in the Northern Sierra of Oaxaca*, by Roberto J. Gonzalez (University of Texas Press, 2001); the poem "Grass," by Mary Oliver; and *Snake Poems: An Aztec Invocation* by Francisco X. Alarcón (collected in *From the Other Side of Night / Del otro lado de la noche*, University of Arizona Press, 2002). Special thanks to Ignacio Chapela for so generously sharing his insights on transgenic contamination in corn.

Ann's Answer
Holding Our Own: The Selected Poems of Ann Stanford, eds. Maxine Scates and David Trinidad (Copper Canyon Press, 2001).

Westerner Exiled to the Affordable Midwest Comes Home
Epigraph from "Vita Nova," in *Vita Nova* by Louise Glück. Copyright © 1999 by Louise Glück. Reprinted by permission of HarperCollins Publishers.

ACKNOWLEDGMENTS

Thank you to the editors of the following publications, in which some of these poems first appeared:

Print

Askew, Barrow Street, BorderSenses, Cipactli, Clan of the Dog, Copper Nickel, Dánta, Ellipsis, Isotope, The Lyric, Mandorla, The Normal School, The Packinghouse Review, Palabra, Pilgrimage, Salt Flats Annual, Solo Café

Online

Maverick, qaartsiluni

Anthologies

Mark My Words: Five Emerging Poets, ed. Francisco Aragón (Momotombo Press, 2001); *Between Water and Song: New Poets for the Twenty-first Century*, ed. Norman Minnick (White Pine Press, 2010); *Mentor and Muse: Essays from Poets to Poets*, eds. Blas Falconer, Beth Martinelli, and Helena Mesa (Southern Illinois University Press, 2010)

For their friendship and careful reading, thank you to Francisco Aragón, Nancy Arora, Kristen Buckles, Steven Cordova, Blas Falconer, Javaughn Fernanders, Gina Franco, Yosefa Raz, and the Splinters.

ABOUT THE AUTHOR

Maria Melendez edits and publishes *Pilgrimage*, a literary magazine in residence at the Nature and Raptor Center of Pueblo emphasizing place, spirit, and witness. She has published two previous collections of poetry: the chapbook *Base Pairs* (Swan Scythe Press, 2001) and *How Long She'll Last in This World* (University of Arizona Press, 2006), which received Honorable Mention at the 2007 International Latino Book Awards and was named a finalist for the 2007 PEN Center USA Literary Awards.

Library of Congress Cataloging-in-Publication Data

Meléndez, María (María Teresa)
  Flexible bones : poems / by María Meléndez.
    p. cm. — (Camino del sol)
  ISBN 978-0-8165-2833-2 (pbk. : alk. paper)
  I. Title.
  PS3613.E446F57 2010
  811'.6—dc22   2009029728

Breinigsville, PA USA
04 February 2010
231956BV00002B/2/P

9 780816 528332